Seeds of a Nation

Alabama

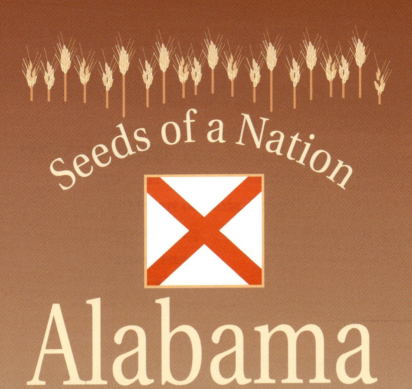

Seeds of a Nation

Alabama

Teresa L. Hyman

KIDHAVEN
PRESS™

THOMSON
━━━━━━━
GALE™

San Diego • Detroit • New York • San Francisco • Cleveland
New Haven, Conn. • Waterville, Maine • London • Munich

© 2004 by KidHaven Press. KidHaven Press is an imprint of The Gale Group, Inc.,
a division of Thomson Learning, Inc.

KidHaven™ and Thomson Learning™ are trademarks used herein under license.

For more information, contact
KidHaven Press
27500 Drake Rd.
Farmington Hills, MI 48331-3535
Or you can visit our Internet site at http://www.gale.com

LIBRARY OF CONGRESS CATALOGING-IN-PUBLICATION DATA
Hyman, Teresa L.
Alabama / by Teresa L. Hyman
p. cm. — (Seeds of a Nation)
Summary: Discusses the early history of Alabama including Native Americans,
European exploration and settlement, and statehood.
Includes bibliographical references and index.
ISBN 0-7377-2079-4 (hardback : alk. paper)
1. Alabama—History—To 1819—Juvenile literature. [1. Alabama—History—
To 1819.] I. Title. II. Series.
F326.3.H96 2004
976.1—dc21
2003010070

Printed in the United States of America

Contents

Chapter One

The First Alabamians

Alabama is a state rich in history and natural resources. It is surrounded by the southern states of Georgia to the east, Tennessee to the north, Mississippi to the west, and Florida just to the south. In addition to these neighbors, Alabama is bordered by the Gulf of Mexico in the southwest corner of the state. The narrow strip of coastline the gulf creates allows Alabama to add beautiful, warm beaches to its list of natural features.

From the Appalachian Highlands to the Gulf Coastal Plain, Alabama boasts lush forests and rivers teeming with wildlife. With average temperatures in the 60s, and a long growing season, Alabama is one of the most temperate and fertile states in the United States. Its mild winters and warm summers attract thousands of visitors each year, and many people retire to the state in order to take advantage of the moderate climate.

Currently, Alabama is ranked twenty-third in population, with more than 4 million people calling the state home in the year 2000. Long before it became a state with a diverse population of people with African, English, French, Irish, and Scottish ancestry, Alabama's original inhabitants were Native Americans.

Early Cultures

Native people arrived in the area now called Alabama in 7000 B.C. These Paleo Indians lived in natural shelters such as caves, and hunted huge, now-extinct animals such as woolly mammoths and bison. They formed

Alabama's Place in the United States Today

crude hunting tools out of rocks and made their simple clothing from the hides of the animals they killed. As generations passed and the giant beasts that roamed the forests died out, the native people began to clear trees in order to grow corn and other vegetables. Scientists call the natives of this newer culture the Archaic Indians.

Archaic Indians hunted smaller animals than their Paleo Indian ancestors. They used spears to kill deer, bears, rabbits, and squirrels. Archaic Indians made spears from rocks, tree limbs, and strings of animal hide or muscle. They also used stones to make drills, chopping tools, knife blades, and fishhooks. In addition to hunting for their food and growing simple vegetables, the Archaic Indians gathered wild berries, fruits, and seeds. They also ate a variety of shellfish.

Both the Paleo Indians and the Archaic Indians were **nomadic**, meaning that instead of making permanent homes and communities, they traveled from place to place in search of food and shelter. Unlike their Paleo Indian relatives, the Archaic Indians practiced prepared burials. They dug graves for their dead and marked the graves with stones.

The Woodland People

About thirty-two hundred to one thousand years ago, the Archaic Indian culture began to change. Their tools and farming practices became more advanced and they relied more heavily on farming. **Archaeologists** call this period of time the Woodland, or Mississippian, Culture. During this time tools such as the bow and arrow were

Paleo Indians hunted woolly mammoths, a now extinct species.

developed. The native people also created needles from stone and animal bones. Their tools allowed them to create leather clothing such as skirts, shirts, and pants. They also made pottery and used dyes from wild berries to decorate the pottery.

The Woodland people depended on farming more than previous cultures. They made hoes and shovels to help plant and tend their crops of corn, squash, and other vegetables. As food became more plentiful, they began to build more permanent homes. Their days as nomads soon ended. The Woodland people also formed tribes as small families began living close together to provide shelter and support one another. Chiefs ruled each of the tribes and decided which tribes would trade with each other. Tribes traded crops, shells, clothing, beads, weapons, tools, and pottery.

During this time, the Woodland people began to build large mounds of earth up to sixty feet high. These mounds were often used as burial sites or places of worship. The activities of the villages and towns were centered around these earth mounds. In fact, mound building became the focus of the Woodland Culture from the years 800 to 1500. The Mississippian people left grave offerings such as decorated pottery at these mounds. Their culture thrived until the mid-1500s.

The Woodland people built mounds of earth like this one as burial sites and places of worship.

Muskogean Tribes

Around the late 1500s and early 1600s, different tribes began to move into the area now known as Alabama. These tribes were made up of smaller native groups that had **migrated** to the region from the East and Midwest. They moved to the Alabama, Mississippi, and Georgia areas to avoid contact with the Europeans who had already entered their lands. These tribes are called Muskogean after the Muskogee language they spoke.

The largest of the Muskogean tribes were the Creek, the Choctaw, and the Chickasaw. The Creek lived in parts of Florida and Georgia as well as Alabama. The state of Alabama gets its name from a group of Creek called the Alibamu, which means "the brush clearers." The Chickasaw lived in the northern portions of Alabama, while the Choctaw lived in southern Alabama along the Tombigbee River.

The Muskogeans farmed the land, raising crops such as tobacco, squash, beans, and corn. In addition to being successful farmers, they were excellent canoe makers. They also made beads and crafts, which were traded among the tribes.

The Muskogean tribes lived in large towns called *italwa*. Each *italwa* was surrounded by smaller villages. In the center of each town was a *pascova,* or plaza, that was used for dancing, ceremonies, and games. Within each *pascova* was a large round building used for tribal meetings. The chief, called a *Mico,* met there with the assistant chief and representatives from the town. A speaker announced the chief's decisions to the rest of the tribe.

Choctaw play a ball game. The Choctaw were one of the Muskogean tribes that settled Alabama in the late sixteenth century.

When a Muskogean town reached four hundred to six hundred people, the town divided. Half the residents moved to a new site and built another *pascova* and meetinghouse. The residents also built new houses and planted crops. The new town remained loyal to the original town. This is how the Muskogean formed **confederacies**. In a Muskogean confederacy, all tribes maintained ties. Tribal chiefs worked together to settle disputes between the towns or between different Muskogean tribes.

The First Alabamians

At the time of the first European explorers, the Muskogean tribes were thriving in Alabama. They had a strong, successful system of government, and their towns and villages boasted high populations and healthy crops. Their way of life was soon disrupted, however, when Spanish explorers stumbled into Choctaw territory.

Chapter Two

Early Explorers

Explorers from Spain were the first Europeans to reach the area of Alabama. They came in search of gold. Although Spaniards were the first to arrive, Alabama was actually settled by the French, who built forts and cities over the large tract of land they called Louisiana.

The Early Spanish Explorers

In 1519 Spanish explorer Alonso Álvarez de Piñeda navigated what is now Mobile Bay, Alabama. Piñeda was on his way from Florida to Mexico when he stopped at what he named the Espíritu Santo river and bay. He stayed in the area for forty days, trading with the local Native Americans and overseeing repairs to his four ships. With new supplies, Piñeda set sail again for Mexico, still mapping the area for future Spanish expeditions. The next Spanish explorer would not only stay in

Alabama for some time, but he would also leave behind a trail of death and destruction.

Hernando de Soto arrived in Alabama in 1540. He and his Spanish expedition landed in Tampa Bay, Florida, looking for gold. Taking almost nine hundred men with him, de Soto marched to Tennessee before heading south to Alabama. Along the journey, de Soto and his men encountered many Native American villages. The Spanish plundered the villages, taking food and clothing,

Hernando de Soto and his men arrive in Florida. They traveled from Florida, through Tennessee, to Alabama in search of gold.

and mistreating the Native Americans with whom they came into contact. Word of the strange new visitors spread so fast among the Native American tribes that the news had reached Alabama long before the men themselves arrived. When de Soto arrived near the village of Mabila in Alabama, the Choctaw tribe and their chief Tuskaloosa attacked the expedition. The largest Indian battle in North America ensued.

Dressed in the traditional armor of Spanish conquistadors, and carrying guns and other European weapons, de Soto's men battled the Choctaw warriors. After several hours of fighting, the village was destroyed, and most of its two thousand residents were dead. The survivors of de Soto's expedition fled Alabama and, by

Spanish conquistadores battle Native Americans. The Spanish plundered every Native American village they encountered.

1543, had made it safely to Mexico. De Soto, however, did not survive the journey. He died along the Mississippi River in 1542.

Searching for Gold

Nineteen years after the bloody war at Mabila, another Spanish explorer came to the Alabama area. Captain Tristan de Luna led one thousand settlers and five hundred soldiers from Mexico to Mobile Bay in an attempt to establish a Spanish **colony**. The colony was supposed to be settled in Florida, but de Luna remained in the area because he was blinded by the thought of gold. He sent half of the soldiers and settlers with his assistant to Florida, while half the party stayed with him at Mobile Bay to search for treasure. Both parties were unsuccessful. A severe storm damaged most of the ships headed for Florida. Those who survived returned to Mobile Bay, where the trips to find gold had left the supplies low and the soldiers and settlers angry. Hunger and disease soon swept through de Luna's expedition. The crew tried to plant crops on the sandy shores of the Alabama River, but the crops were unable to grow in those conditions. In 1561, after a harsh winter, the settlers and soldiers revolted against de Luna. They abandoned their efforts to establish a colony and look for gold, and returned to Mexico.

Unexpected Results

The Spanish were not able to start a permanent colony, but their presence in Alabama had a lasting effect on the native people living there. Diseases brought by the explorers, such as smallpox and influenza, killed thousands of Native Americans and even wiped out whole tribes. Smaller tribes such as the Hitchiti, Alibamu, Tuskegee, and Koasati needed protection from the Europeans and hostile Native American tribes. They also needed help growing food for their people. These small tribes combined with the Creek to become part of the Creek Confederacy.

The Cherokee, another Native American tribe, also came to live near the Creek in Alabama and Georgia. The Cherokee were forced from their homelands in Tennessee, North Carolina, and South Carolina by English settlers and the diseases they carried. When the French came to Alabama in the late 1600s, they encountered Native Americans from the Creek Confederacy, the Choctaw and Chickasaw tribes, as well as the Cherokee.

The French Arrive

The French government knew that Spain was having success in the areas now known as Florida and Mexico. France had already established itself in the northern areas of the New World—now called Canada—but did not want to miss an opportunity in the South. In 1679, France sent its own explorer, René-Robert Cavelier La Salle, to the southern territories of the New World. La Salle claimed all land surrounding the Mississippi River for France. He named the new territory Louisiana to honor the French king Louis XIV. As a reward for his efforts, La Salle was given more ships, more men, and a

Forced from their lands, Indian tribes came to Alabama to become part of the Creek Confederacy.

challenging new mission. France wanted him to sail to the Gulf of Mexico, invade the Spanish territory, and take whatever gold he could find. La Salle's mission was unsuccessful, however. He was killed in Texas on March 19, 1687, during a mutiny. Despite this setback, France sent more explorers to the southern lands of the New World.

Nine years after La Salle claimed the Louisiana territory for France, two brothers established the first French settlement in what is now Mississippi. Born in Montreal in what we now call Canada, Pierre and Jean-Baptiste Le Moyne were officers in the French navy. They were chosen by the French Minister of Marine to explore the area surrounding the Mississippi River and establish a colony in Louisiana. Sailing from Brest,

René-Robert Cavelier La Salle claims land for France. He named the area Louisiana.

France, on October 24, 1698, the Le Moyne expedition landed near Cat Island off the coast of Mississippi on February 13, 1699. Days later, on February 27, the brothers took two birch canoes and forty-eight men to explore the Mississippi and Red Rivers. They returned to the ship, and, with the crew, built a fort called Marepas, or Old Biloxi, on the northeast side of the Bay of Biloxi in Mississippi.

After other French settlers arrived, Fort Louis of Mobile was built. This was the first French settlement in what is now Alabama. The city of Mobile rose many years later just twenty-five miles from this site. The French, unfortunately, were not prepared for the warm, humid climate or the different soil conditions of the new territory. The crops the settlers planted failed, and soon they were on the brink of starvation. Disease also ran rampant through the settlement. These problems almost brought an end to Fort Louis. In 1711, a flood destroyed the fort and the Le Moyne brothers moved the settlers from the Mobile River farther south to the mouth of Mobile Bay.

Fort Condé

When the new fort, Fort Condé, was constructed in 1720, the French built a relationship with the surrounding Native American tribes. The French began trading with the neighboring Choctaw. The French traded European blankets, cooking utensils, and clothing for animal skins and furs. In addition to supplying the French settlers with animal pelts that could be sold in France for high prices, the Choctaw

Pierre Le Moyne and his brother helped establish the first French settlement in Alabama.

also gave the French food and showed them improved farming techniques.

Although it teetered on the edge of failure, the French settlement at Fort Condé succeeded and eventually became the city of Mobile, Alabama. The French built other settlements in the Louisiana territory, but could not keep their hold on the land. They would eventually give up control of the territory to England, and the English and Americans would develop it.

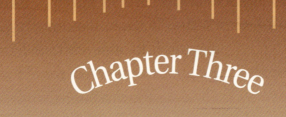

Chapter Three

Settlers

The French worked hard to ensure the success of their settlement in Louisiana. In spite of their attempts, however, the French would lose control of Louisiana after a bloody war with Britain and its Native American **allies**. Alabama would eventually benefit from this loss.

Early Settlements

In 1704, the French government sent two dozen women from France to Mobile to marry the male colonists. The government wanted them to start families in the new territory and settle there, making the colony more stable. With additional mouths to feed, the colonists needed more money. So they grew crops they could sell to Europe. These included sugar and indigo, a plant used to make a dark, bluish purple dye.

As the colonists expanded their fields, the need for more workers also grew. They brought in six hundred

French colonists brought African slaves to Alabama to work in their fields.

African slaves in 1719. Between trading with the Choctaw and selling their own crops, the settlers experienced improvements in daily life at Fort Condé. In 1717 the French built Fort Toulouse on the Coosa River to provide another trading location. Fort Toulouse also had another purpose—to keep an eye on the British. British colonists had begun to settle on land belonging to France, and they had begun to trade with the Native Americans in the territory as well. The French saw this as a threat. Skirmishes between the British and the French soon took place. Eventually, war erupted between them. Called the French and Indian War, its battles were fought all over the new territory. When France was defeated in 1763, it turned over all its land east of the Mississippi, including what is now Alabama, to the British.

The British and the Americans

During Britain's short rule, several British colonists established homesteads along stretches of Alabama's rivers. These newcomers were of Irish, Scottish, and English ancestry and came to the new territory from British colonies in the East. These new settlers had

British and French soldiers fight in the French and Indian War. At the end of the war, France surrendered Alabama to England.

learned farming techniques from Native Americans in New England, Virginia, and the Carolinas. They successfully grew corn, squash, and beans, as well as cash crops such as tobacco and cotton.

Over the next forty years, Alabama fell under the control of the British, the Spanish, and, once again, the French. In 1803, France sold land to the United States in a sale called the Louisiana Purchase. With this sale, Alabama was finally under American control.

Americans quickly began moving to Alabama to search for new, fertile farmlands. These new settlers encountered the Cherokee, the Chickasaw, and the Choctaw, as well as the Creek. At first these Native American tribes tolerated the white settlers, and even adopted certain European customs such as the English language and style of dress. However, as more settlers arrived, they began to take more Native American land. Fearing that the new settlers would displace them totally, several tribes rebelled against the newcomers.

The Creek War

In the early 1800s, a Shawnee chief named Tecumseh traveled across the country speaking to different Native American tribes. According to Tecumseh, the European settlers were greedy and would never rest until they took away all Native American lands. In 1813, under the influence of Tecumseh's teachings, several Creek tribes took up arms against the settlers. One such group was the Red Stick Creek. They wore red face or body paint, or wore head coverings colored red, the Muskogean

The Louisiana Purchase

British North America

Oregon Country

Massachusetts
Vermont
New Hampshire
New York
Rhode Island
Connecticut
New Jersey
Pennsylvania
Delaware
Maryland
North Carolina
South Carolina

Louisiana Purchase 1803

Indiana Territory
Ohio
Virginia
Kentucky
Tennessee
Mississippi Territory
Georgia

New Spain

Spanish Florida

Current State Boundaries

color for war. Their chiefs even carried bundles of twigs painted red to show their dedication to war. These Red Stick Creek waged a war against the newly formed United States in an attempt to keep their lands.

In July of 1813, the Red Stick Creek and the Americans engaged in a bloody battle near Belleville, Alabama. While fighting the battle at Burnt Corn Creek, the Creek forced the Americans to retreat to a nearby fort. On August 30, the Creek attacked the fort, killing most of the white settlers, including women and children. In response, Andrew Jackson, then a leader in the U.S. Army, was sent from Tennessee to put an end to the Creek War.

In 1814 Jackson and his soldiers fought their way from Tennessee to Alabama. They killed any Native

Shawnee chief Tecumseh urged Native American tribes to fight the European settlers.

Americans they encountered, even those of tribes not loyal to the Red Sticks, and burned many villages. When the Americans finally reached the Tallapoosa River, where the Red Sticks were camped, a four-hour battle took place. Menawa, the leader of the Red Sticks, was defeated. Jackson forced all the tribes in the Creek Confederacy, even those who did not fight in the Creek War, to sign over all their land to the United States. The Americans now had complete control over the territory known as Louisiana.

Cotton Is King

As Creek land opened up to white settlers, Alabama's population exploded. Settlers were attracted to the rich soil and abundant wildlife. They came from Virginia, Tennessee, Georgia, and North Carolina and began growing cotton in huge amounts. Soon, cotton **plantations** sprang up throughout the territory. The rich, dark soil of central and southern Alabama was ideal for growing cotton. However, the soil was hard to plow. Owners of large farms used African slaves to plow, plant, and handpick the cotton at harvest time. The plantation owners made large sums of money selling the cotton to nearby mills. These mills spun the cotton into cloth and sold the cloth to clothing companies and small general stores.

The fabric industry created many jobs in the territory. In 1802, Alabama's first **cotton gin**, a machine that made it faster and easier to separate the cotton seed from the cotton fiber, helped increase cotton production. More jobs were created as plantation owners planted

Slaves operate a cotton gin. Alabama's soil was ideal for growing cotton.

more crops and harvested more cotton. Farmhands were hired to help keep the plantations running smoothly and to keep the slaves producing. Wagon makers were needed to provide transportation for the cotton from the plantations to the mills. More mills were built to keep up with the increase in cotton. Spinners, weavers, and cotton gin operators were hired to keep up with production. Blacksmiths and machinists were needed to keep the mills running and to keep the plantations supplied with farming tools. More settlers came to Alabama in search of new opportunities.

As the cotton industry created more jobs for the settlers, towns and cities such as Huntsville and Montgomery sprang up. So many people began to arrive in the territory that the government needed to search for ways to handle the growing population.

Chapter Four

The Twenty-Second State

Many Americans and European immigrants were attracted to the Louisiana territory. Soon, the government divided the large region into more manageable sections. This paved the way for Alabama to find its own identity and become a state.

A Growing Population

In 1813, only about twelve thousand Europeans and African slaves lived in what is now Alabama. By 1819, due to the success of the cotton industry, that number had soared to more than 130,000. Many Americans as well as European immigrants from Ireland, Scotland, and France flocked to the territory in search of a better life. Jobs were plentiful. Due to the end of the Creek War, there were few conflicts with Native Americans. Another plus for the new territory was the development of schools and new businesses.

Because of the booming cotton industry, Alabama's population soared in the early 1800s.

In 1811, Washington Academy in Mobile was established to provide a more structured education to the large numbers of children who came with their parents to the territory. Green Academy in the new city of Huntsville opened the following year. Prominent white settlers sent their children to these schools. Children of less prosperous farming families were either educated at home, or at smaller, neighboring schoolhouses. African slaves who lived in the territory were not permitted any form of education.

Booming Businesses

New businesses and industries quickly developed in larger towns such as Montgomery. Plantation owners, fabric manufacturers, and general-store owners came to Montgomery to bargain for the best prices on cotton, goods, and services. Lawyers set up offices to assist in these trade agreements. Bankers and doctors opened offices in the city as well. Soon bakers, tailors, dressmakers, and cobblers set up shops to provide services to the growing number of settlers who visited the city. This kind of growth happened in trade areas all over the territory.

The slave trade also boomed in the territory. Plantation owners needed slaves to perform the grueling work of raising and picking cotton. Slaves also kept tobacco and vegetable farms running. Buying and selling slaves grew into a big business as slave traders brought their human cargo to the territory and farmers sold, bought, and traded their slaves.

The development of the iron and steamboat industries also helped bring more settlers to the region. In 1818 the Cedar Creek Furnace opened in what is now Franklin County, and Alabama began to produce iron in large amounts. That same year, the area's first steamboat, *The Alabama*, was manufactured in St. Stephens. The iron and boatbuilding industries created new jobs and attracted craftsmen such as blacksmiths and shipbuilders to the region.

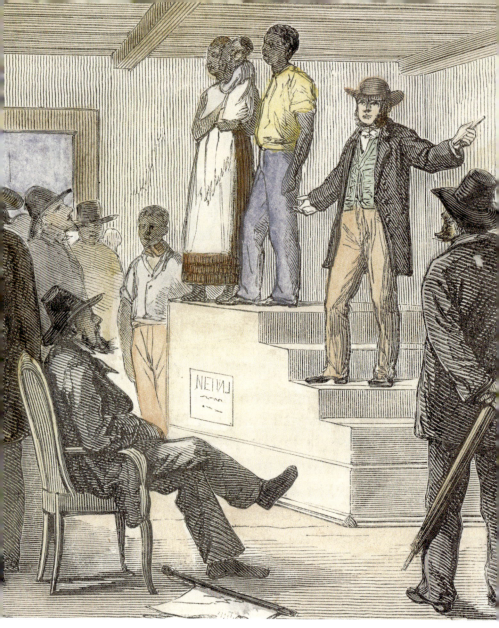

A slave trader sells a slave family. The slave trade was a big business in Alabama.

Seeking Statehood

The new territory grew rapidly, and the U.S. government did not want to lose out on money coming to this region. The successful businesses in the territory offered a source of money for the United States. As long as it remained a territory, however, the government could not tax the large shipping, cotton, and iron ore businesses. In March of 1817, Congress divided the Mississippi territory and admitted Mississippi as the twentieth state. The less-populated area of the territory was named Alabama. It remained a territory, but its settlers quickly began to organize their government and seek statehood.

From 1817 to 1819, Alabama's population grew so steadily that President James Monroe signed an enabling act on March 2, 1819. This act was the first step in making Alabama a state. Once Alabama had sixty thousand people, a working government, and new businesses it could become a state. Citizens of the territory desperately wanted statehood. They wanted to benefit from the laws of the United States and the rights it gave its citizens. The citizens voted for lawmakers to help them work through the process of becoming a state. These lawmakers worked quickly to establish a government for the territory.

The First Legislature

On January 19, 1818, the first **legislature** of the Alabama territory met in St. Stephens, Alabama, at the Douglass Hotel. The first order of business for the newly formed legislature was to decide on a capital for the territory. Each representative wanted the capital to be located in or near his home city. Because the legislators could not agree on a location, they created a brand new town. The town of Cahaba was established at the intersection of the Cahaba

President James Monroe helped Alabama become a state.

and Alabama Rivers to act as the capital of Alabama. Cahaba remained the capital of Alabama until 1826, when the capital was moved to Tuscaloosa. Even after that move, legislators were not in agreement with the site of the capital. The capital was changed from Tuscaloosa to Montgomery in 1846, and has remained there ever since. After the first legislators established the capital, they turned their attention toward developing a state constitution.

Meeting in a cabinetmaker's shop in the city of Huntsville, legislators drafted the Alabama state constitution. In July of 1819, legislators quickly **ratified** the constitution.

Becoming a State

In September of 1819, the people of the Alabama territory elected their first governor. In the close election, William Wyatt Bibb, a former Georgia doctor, received

Montgomery became Alabama's capital in 1846. The state capitol building is seen here.

8,342 votes while his opponent received 7,140 votes. The governor's main duty during his term of office was to set up the Alabama state government. Governor Bibb appointed an attorney general to make sure the laws of the territory were communicated to the settlers and enforced. Governor Bibb organized the Alabama militia and helped to organize the state supreme court, which began to operate in May of 1820. Bibb also initiated the construction of state buildings, streets, and roads. Although Governor Bibb helped lay the foundations for the Alabama state government, he would not live to see some of his work fulfilled. While in office, Bibb received multiple internal injuries after a fall from his horse. He contracted tuberculosis and died July 9, 1820.

On December 14, 1819, the U.S. Congress voted to admit Alabama into the Union. It became the twenty-second state of the United States of America. Its diverse population, abundance of natural resources, and its growing businesses and industries added to the beauty and prosperity of the budding new country.

Facts About Alabama

State motto: *Audemus Jura Nostra Defendere* ("We Dare Defend Our Rights")

State song: "Alabama" by Julia S. Tutwiler

State nicknames: Heart of Dixie, Yellowhammer State

State capital: Montgomery

Largest city: Birmingham

Population in 2000: 4,447,100

Number of counties: 67

Lowest point: Gulf of Mexico

Highest point: Cheaha Mountain (2,407 feet)

State flower: camellia

State bird: yellowhammer (yellow-shafted flicker)

State horse: racking horse

State butterfly: eastern tiger swallowtail

State insect: monarch butterfly

State reptile: red-bellied turtle

State amphibian: Red Hills salamander

State rock: marble

State mineral: red iron ore

State gemstone: star blue quartz

State tree: southern longleaf pine

State nut: pecan

Famous people: Hank Aaron, baseball player; Charles Barkley, basketball player; Hugo Black, U.S. Supreme Court judge; Jimmy Buffett, musician; W.E. Butterworth, writer; Truman Capote, writer; George Washington Carver, scientist/educator; Nat "King" Cole, singer/pianist; Courtney Cox Arquette, actress; Bo Jackson, professional football and baseball player; Mae C. Jemison, astronaut; Helen Keller, educator/activist; Coretta Scott King, activist; Carl Lewis, track-and-field athlete; Joe Louis, boxer; Willie Mays, baseball player.

Glossary

allies: People or governments who are loyal to one another.

archaeologists: Scientists who study past human lives, cultures, and activities.

colony: A group of people living in a new settlement but ruled by the country that organized the settlement.

confederacy: Groups that join together to support each other.

cotton gin: A machine invented by Eli Whitney that separates the seeds and hulls from cotton fiber.

legislature: An organized body having the authority to make laws.

migrate: To move from one place to another, often for food or because of changes in weather.

nomadic: Roaming from place to place.

plantations: Large farms usually worked by laborers.

ratified: Approved.

For Further Exploration

Books

Virginia Van der Veer Hamilton, *Alabama: A History*. New York: W.W. Norton, 1984. Focuses on the people of Alabama, from its early Native American tribes to white settlers to black slaves and their descendants who ushered in the Civil Rights movement of the 1960s.

Ellen Lloyd Trover, *Alabama: A Chronology and Documentary Handbook*. New York: Oceana Publications, 1972. A reference of basic dates in the history of the state of Alabama, from 1528 until 1970.

Websites

Class Brain (www.classbrain.com). Great website for students and their parents. Everything from informational links for the fifty United States and the U.S. territories to study aids, puzzles, and clip art. Great resource for report finding, book searching, or test preparation.

Creek Indian Bibliography (www.rhus.com). A website bibliography offering resources for information regarding the Creek Nation. Excellent source for research into the history of the Creek Confederacy.

Creek Nation (www.ocevnet.org). Website for the Creek Nation. Focuses on current issues, but has a wealth of historical information about the Creek Nation and its members.

For Further Exploration

Official Website of the Alabama Legislature (www. legislature.state.al.us). Details the six different constitutions of the state of Alabama.

State House Girls (www.statehousegirls.net). A comprehensive website of facts and information about the fifty states, including government links and interesting social and cultural listings for each state.

University of Southern Alabama Archaeology (www. southalabama.edu). Great website for students. Offers biographical profiles of early Alabama colonists.

Index

Picture Credits

About the Author

A native of Tarboro, North Carolina, Teresa L. Hyman is a professional editor and writer living in Overland Park, Kansas. She and her husband, Derrick, are the parents of two children, Briana and Devin. Hyman enjoys researching her Native American and African American heritage and studying the literature and art of those cultures.